Neighbour
Procedure

Neighbour Procedure

Rachel Zolf

COACH HOUSE BOOKS

 Canadä

Published with the generous assistance of the Canada Council for the Arts and the Ontario Arts Council. Coach House Books also acknowledges the support of the Government of Canada through the Book Publishing Industry Development Program and the Government of Ontario through the Ontario Book Publishing Tax Credit.

LIBRARY AND ARCHIVES CANADA CATALOGUING IN PUBLICATION

Zolf, Rachel
    Neighbour procedure / Rachel Zolf. -- 1st ed.

Poems.
ISBN 978-1-55245-229-5

    I. Title.

PS8599.O627N45 2010   C811'.54   C2010-900029-3

Shoot
& Weep

Assaf Balak Barak
Ben Ami Ben Num
Ben Num B Chametz
Chorev Dani Dekel
Gideon Harel Hiram
Horev   Jephtha
Jevuss   Kedem Kil
shon   Maccabee
Mateh   Misparayim
Nachshon   Schfifon
Yiftach Yoav Yoram
Ovda Suzannah Musk
eteer Slope Kadesh
Machbesh   Omer
Steamroller   Focus
Boxer Bulmus   6
Raviv   Drizzle
Rooster 53   Wrath
of God Gazelle Nickel
        Grass   Nimbus
   Moon Moon Water
Nimbus Spar Nimbus
Star Nimbus Stream
Spring   of Youth
Thunderbolt Yonatan
Litani Opera   Peace
for Galilee   Bramble

Bush   Accountability
Grapes   of   Wrath
Picturesque   Journey
Defensive Shield
   Determined Path
   Days of Penitence
Road Closed Rainbow
Purple Iron Brothers
Dwell Just
Reward Change
of Direction Summer
Rains Truthful Prom
ise Cast Lead Cast
Promise   Truthful
Rains Summer Dire
ction of Change Re
ward Just Dwell
Brothers
Iron Purple Rainbow
Closed Road Pen
itence of Days Path
   Determined Shield
Defensive Journey
 Picturesque Wrath of
Grapes   Account
ability Bush Bramble
Galilee   for   Peace

Opera   Litani
Yonatan Thunderbolt
Youth of Spring
   Stream Nimbus Star
Nimbus Spar Nimbus
Water Moon Moon
   Nimbus Grass Nickel
Gazelle God of Wrath
        53   Rooster
   Drizzle Raviv 6
   Bulmus   Boxer
Focus   Steamroller
Omer   Machbesh
Kadesh   Slope
Musketeer Suzannah
Ovda   Yoram   Yoav
   Yiftach Schfifon
        Nachshon Mis
parayim   Mateh
Maccabee   Kilshon
Kedem Jevuss Jep
htha Horev Hir
   am Harel Gideon
Dekel   Dani   Chor
ev Chametz B Num B
en Num Ben Ami Ben
Barak Balak Assaf

'… feel compelled to learn how to say these names?'

– Judith Butler
Precarious Life: The Powers of
Mourning and Violence

a priori

If the Sabbath is a form of constraint

If jihād is the first word learned

If Elie Wiesel is the Holocaust

If one must expropriate gently

If messianism licks at the edges of thought

If the truth does not lie in silence

If naf is self and brother

If the space between two words can be bridged

If moderate physical pressure is acceptable

If the primary target is the witness

If epistemological mastery is an uncloseable wound

If bittahon was trust in God now military security

If there is horror at the heart of divinity

If the body goes off near the Sbarro pizzeria

If the apocalyptic sting is gone from Hebrew

If the first stage is not knowing at all

If this state is the golden calf

If ingathering means expulsion

If catastrophe becomes a passion

If we shoot and weep

If Israel is not in Israel

If the treasure house of well-worn terms is laden with explosives

If ha'apalah was catastrophic breakthrough now illegal immigration

If the bodies of the exploding martyrs smell of musk

If every breath of fresh air is a border

If the state no longer decides who lives or dies

If some are eternally innocent and good

If a key is an archival artifact

If the planes return safely

If they are all enthusiasm

If you are Hamas

If one is Israel

If cruel history repeats itself as its own cure

If it happens inside the Sbarro pizzeria

If there is invasion of the order of the border

If the animal is discomforted during slaughter

If the band of the blind plays and refreshments served

If the third stage is but what can be done

If shahīd is martyr and witness

If preventative is energetic liquidation

If some are a community of fate

If we will and it is a fairy tale

If Sbarro

Did not participate in hostilities

When she approached the barrier

While flying a kite at the beach

When he picked grass for his flock

While sitting in the tin-covered dīwān

When she crossed the street

While on the way to buy candy

When trying to find work

While at home eating supper

While collecting scrap metal with his brother

While fixing the water container during curfew

When on duty in a cement factory

While grazing the flock with two children

When he drew a lighter in the shape of a pistol

Playing outdoors

Near the zoo

During a demonstration

Restoring the ancient palace

Standing next to her window

Serving customers in his butchery

Treating the wounded

Harvesting olives

With a group of children on a hill

Wandering about

Directing traffic

In the field

Near a house

On a motorcycle

In her mother's arms

At a flying checkpoint

On his way to work

On her way to school

With two fishermen on their way back to shore

Coming home from prayers at five in the morning

The neighbour procedure

The neighbour goes in first

I asked my neighbour where the shouting came from

They took me to another neighbour's home

We go through the whole house with the neighbour

At four in the morning I heard my neighbour calling me

The neighbour doesn't have that option

We were seven metres from the neighbour's house

The neighbour shouts, knocks on the door

They ordered my neighbour to bring out the wounded man

My neighbour replied the sound came from my home

When he opened the door his neighbour was standing there

When I opened the door I saw my neighbour in the doorway

The barber

One soldier danced into the shop, 'Nice, nice'

Whose faces were painted certain images don't appear

Cutting in random lines the machine touched my scalp

Can you be gentle I'm not an expert open your mouth

A group of children stones his weapon on my shoulder

Intolerable eruption patting his chest, 'Now I'll tell you my name'

Sometimes staccato sometimes continuous

The soldier left the barbershop with the scissors

The soldier left the hair on my lips

We have to make you do a little sports

Me, I got the call up, 'Great, let's go beat the shit out of them'

A stinking sack on my head and cuffs marked 'Made in England'

A stone thrown at total awareness tells night from day

By certain signs they called my number but you can't chop wood

Without splinters tied to the chair, 'I'm going to dirty my hands'

Aware of the risk these phrases stop vehicles passing by

I don't like criticism from high-souled people losing track of time

Not a good idea for us two clubs broke embarrassed suit doesn't fit

'He's got a pain in his heart' raining with strong winds

95 percent of the work shouldn't involve pangs three or four metres back

Of a big blue conscience I can't talk to you gently

If we don't hurry people will die closed inside hell we're Jews

We've been through the Shoah to forget all the time somehow

The holy national interest confessed to distributing leaflets

The quiet of the night took the piece of white paper and left the room

The lone soldier

Lone soldiers don't get visits from Mom and Dad

Came from Connecticut. Alone

No nation on earth that is more lonely

Came from Qallabat. Alone

Don't have a brother to our coping

Don't have a sister to our escape

No partner to immobilization

Supposed to get wings and fly off on your own

It means Mom can't bake a cake for my army buddies

Means coming home before Shabbat and doing laundry

A book with no cover

I prayed I'd receive

Can't even express

Being a lone soldier means being alone

But Baltimore should know you're not alone

A helping hand extended. A hug Siberia

Like a Casablanca medal

Serving is the most Israeli part

With you, Ukraine. Now and forever

Thank you to all of Ekaterinburg's picks

Coin of the realm is U.S. brain- and heart-power

Putting yourself forward on the Tehran line for

Our quality in South African human resources

These are the kind Canada wants to be made of

Many lonely hearts one Great Library

Chief Booklover's weeps guaranteed at the end

The capacity to give names

Nahal arose in the place of Mahalul

Kibbutz Gvat in the place of Jibta

Kibbutz Sarid in the place of Huneifis

Ein Houd turned into Ein Hod

Al-Ghazzawiyya now Ma'oz Chayyim

Alumma instead of Hatta

Ruchama on top of al-Jammama

Kefer Warburg in lieu of Qastina

Shahar stands in for al-Faluja

Ma'anit in the shoes of Wadi 'Ara

Gal-On stepped into Ra'na

Nurit substituted for Nuris

Nachalat Jabotinsky supplanted al-Shuna

Yizre'el squatted on Zir'in

Najd succumbed to Sderot

Bayt Nattif pinned by Roglit

Saffuriyya quashed by Hosha'aya

Tel Aviv cut out al-Shaykh Muwannis

Canada Park grafted onto Imwas

Staim burrowed into al-Burayl

Ameilim nullified Abu Shusha

Gan Soreq consumed al-Nabi Rubin

Jimzu demolished by Gimzo

Kibbutz Sha'alvirn snuffed Salbit

Ziqim extinguished Hiribya

Bashshit devoured by Kannot

Na'an lay waste to al-Na'ani

Yavne struck at the heart of Yibna

Al-Dawayima shattered by Amatzya

Kibbutz Birriya made short work of Birriya

'Alma laid axe to the root of 'Alma

Zarnuqa ravaged Zarnuqa with fire and sword

A certain kind of madness

Little town of Bayt Lahm in barbed wire and concrete

We'll be friends and I'll help you clog the throat

The bulldozer uprooted each deed and thought big

The doctor stuck the stethoscope through the gap

No continuity between ground and sky

The border churning documents with the soil

Apache in the air, Caterpillar on earth

Crust and subterrain

The baby's head crowned in the corridor

Land flattened, turns to a neighbouring field

Run from the depressing tin huts to pick some last oranges

At the gate

What's with this donkey tying the rope to the jeep

Told me to wear the saddle's leg fell off and it roamed around

Ride to the greenhouse narrative faltering put it on my shoulders

Hands bound no beauty here just a donkey with three legs

I'll chase you to make a long story short get rid of it

The saddle still on my back I forget its name

This one's a potential explosive donkey go fuck it

An hour later negated lives have a strange way of remaining animated

The donkey's back lifting the tail and tying it around

My head led the donkey aside and shot it in the head

I stood behind the tail too short: 'enough'

His weapon

Thirty minutes

I tried to look

We must attend

Losing what we can't fully fathom

Then he tightened the saddle and returned my ID

Harming families has proven an effective policy

I am illiterate and a widow and everything came as a surprise

By the power vested in Regulation 1 1 9 the abstract rises up and destroys the real

The Molotov terrorist's grandmother did not show me a decree

The engineer took a tape measure and a hole gapes in the familiar space

One shove and a favour of five minutes to remove belonging

I saved the oil and some of a Red Cross tent

While the living turns into an incident that took two hours

Declare this my signature forbidden to smash the sealed openings

car bomb car bomb car bomb car bomb car bomb
truck bomb car bomb car bomb truck bomb
suitcase bomb car bomb *calmo* car bombs car bomb
car bomb car bomb mule bomb car bomb car bomb
car bomb car bomb car bomb *a piacere* car bomb car
bomb grenades mule bomb car bomb car bomb car
bomb car bomb car bomb car bomb *rest* car bomb
belt bomb *mf* belt bomb bike bomb *pressez* belt bomb
belt bomb car bombs car bomb mule bomb belt
bomb belt bomb *rest* belt bomb belt bomb belt bomb
belt bomb *ritenuto* belt bomb belt bomb belt bomb *mp*
bike bomb belt bomb belt *a tempo* bomb belt bomb belt
bomb belt bomb belt *accelerando* bomb belt bomb belt
bomb belt bomb truck bomb *sempre* car bomb belt
bomb belt bomb belt bomb *crescendo* car bomb belt
bomb car bomb belt bomb belt bomb *animando* belt
bomb belt bomb car *poco* bomb car bomb *a* car bomb
poco belt bomb *allegro* belt bomb *mf* belt bomb belt bomb
belt bomb belt *forte* bomb belt bomb bag bomb belt
bomb belt bomb *vivo* car bomb belt bomb belt *espressivo*
bomb belt bomb belt *ff* bomb belt bomb belt bomb
molto belt bomb belt bomb belt bomb belt *fff* bomb belt
bomb belt bomb *ffff* car bomb suitcase bomb *fff* belt
bomb belt *diminuendo* bomb belt bomb belt bomb car *ff*
bomb belt bomb belt bomb belt *rallentando* bomb *f* bag
bombs belt bomb belt bomb belt bomb belt *mf* bomb
belt *passionato* bomb car bomb belt bomb belt bomb
bag bomb belt bomb belt bomb *poco* belt *mp* bomb belt
bomb belt bomb belt bomb belt *p* bomb *a* belt bomb
perdendo bike bomb bag bomb *poco* belt bomb belt
bomb *pp* belt bomb *ritardando* belt bomb belt bomb belt
cédez bomb belt bomb belt bomb *ppp* belt bomb
belt bomb belt bomb *pppp* belt *ppppp* bomb

A failure of hospitality

I had normal dreams like wires dangling everywhere

The ludicrous thing about order won't hear lies only peace

Her body full with splinters can't pick the olives alone

Luxurious character of the negative raised a lion in your house

No Hebrew word for integrity will be a blazing light

Future collapsed in present execution and mourning

Duty of guest and host a torn native

Narratives compete for a sacred hair lying where it shouldn't

Stoked button the key to distilled water living a quiet way

This unbearable intimacy a purity of arms suturing

Chocolate cake with coconut flecks none of us taught to see

Besieged body a piece of metal we will offer all our children

This permanent remembrance slaughtered and we promise a pleasant life

Grievable

Du'aa Naser Saleh 'Abd al-Qader

Zaher Jaber Muhammad al-Majdalawi

Ghanem Khalil Muhammad al-Khatib

Jihad 'Abd al-Majid Isma'il al-Hayah

'Aiyadah Dahud Pathiya

Abir Bassam 'Abd Rab al-'Alamin

Nizar Raji 'Abdallah 'Obeid

Fatma Muhammad Hussein

Ma'sud Rajab Muhammad Subuh

'Anan Muhammad Ass'ad al-Tibi

Hamadah Mahmoud Jamal al-Fiyumi

Sarah Suliman 'Abdallah Abu Ghazal

Rakan 'Abed Kayed Nsserat

Rizeq Ziad Rizeq Musleh

Hamed Yasin Hamed Bahlul

Islam Hashem Razaq Zaharan

Wahib Musleh Nayef al-Dik

Bushara Naji Wahsh Barjis

Rami Samir Nayef Shana'ah

Zin al-'Aabdin Muhammad Mahmoud Shahin

Radeh 'Iyesha

'Abd al-Karim Khaled Salem Zaharan

Mustafa Hamdan 'Abd al-Qader Ramlawi

Ikrami Ghaleb Nimer Abu 'Amshah

Ikram Barhum Salman Qadih

Adib Salim Ibrahim Ahmad

Wa'el Taleb Muhammad Nassar

Iman Muhammad Haju

Kamela Muhammad As'ad al-Shuli

Sa'id Salem Suleiman Hajjaj

Najwa 'Awad Rajab Khalif

Hamdan Muhammad Hamdan Barhum

Muhammad Mahmoud Rajab al-Jarjawi

At five o'clock in the morning

Nominal

14

13

33

17

42

10

17

65

21

52

15

8

15

16

16

14

28

seventeen

twenty five

thirty five

eighteen

fifteen

forty one

twenty three

twenty two

thirty eight

thirty eight

under one

twenty

twenty

twenty four

twenty

nineteen

at 5

Loss has made a tenuous we

A touch of the worst border my wound testifies

Names must break up and flatten my foreignness to myself

One is hit by implements given over without control

Exhausted not knowing why beauty is left of me what hair

Fathom who have wires in the other I have lost

Neighbour renews itself in the inexhaustible

Violence a sudden address from oil

Enthusiasm impressed upon concept

Impinging splinters oneself fallen

Mark that is no uniform

Write open and unbounded gap

Undone by the seal of the other

You are what I gain through this disorientation

Waiting Interrogation Waiting Interrogation Waiting Interrogation Waiting Rest Waiting Interrogation Rest Waiting Interrogation Waiting Interrogation Waiting Interrogation Rest Waiting Interrogation Waiting Interrogation Waiting Interrogation Rest Waiting Interrogation Waiting Interrogation Waiting Interrogation Rest Waiting Interrogation Waiting Interrogation Waiting Interrogation Waiting Interrogation Waiting Rest Waiting Interrogation Waiting Rest Waiting Interrogation Waiting Interrogation Waiting Interrogation Waiting Interrogation Waiting Interrogation Waiting Rest Waiting Interrogation Waiting Interrogation Waiting Interrogation Waiting Rest Waiting Interrogation Rest Waiting Interrogation Waiting Interrogation Waiting Interrogation Rest Waiting Interrogation Waiting Interrogation Waiting Interrogation Rest Waiting Interrogation Waiting Interrogation Waiting Interrogation Waiting Interrogation Rest Waiting Interrogation Waiting Interrogation Waiting Interrogation Waiting Rest Waiting Interrogation Waiting Rest Waiting Interrogation Waiting Interrogation Waiting Interrogation Waiting Interrogation Waiting Interrogation Waiting Rest

terror not frighten thee," and my r;
thee while arguing with thee, and begi

with thee. Cf. the Arabic expressions:
for a light-minded and fickle person.

אכר. אכר (*ib.* 51.23) = أَكَّار, "till
derived from أُكْرَة, "ditch."

אל = إِلَى, "to;" also in Hebrew it
(Jb 29.19); with pronominal suffixes
e.g. אליו, אליך, אליהם, and אליה;
preposition עַל. Of the same root

Book of
Comparisons

19.9

to set

     (start, sun)

west

       she departed

raven

     antishemi

willow   an Arab

       the Arabs

       a pledge

16.22

to pick

glean

          gleanings

               from caataastropha fruit trees

     that

           fell to the ground

30.4

to tie, bind

        I bound the man (with a platfoos strap)

      how well he fastened

his hypoteti pack saddle

                this appellation clung

30.32

black

    charcoal

veeroos

    metaphorically similar

to hover round about

    (bird)

circling

    the basic meaning then baalon

    (clinika wall)

encompassing a city

21.18

nose-

partition

perforated

So-and-so was cut off

by amboolaance

death

declare

unlawful

amerrika

sacred

14.3

they united

became intimately acquainted

I shall adorn homogueni

(speech)

similar to

forrmali gueometria composition

scar of a wound

there is no hair on her head

spots in the leopard's fur

soft hair, fur

16.26

to commit an offence

in my crrem opinion

similar to Arabic

        be light

          light-minded

     for his mouth was guaamaal claatch

                     of the same meaning

       =

my cleptomaan rashness

          let it not be heavy upon thee

          let my terror not frighten thee

8.17

denominative slengue

from

Jew

to repent

return to good

22.12

        gathering together

   teorria waters

       where faiter people assemble

I made the spearheads thin

thin points

29.2

thin bread

      thinness

          saliva

               Thou does not let me swallow my nostaalguia

               I allowed caazaanoba to swallow his saliva

11.9

to throw

into
virtuaali disorder

the confusion of

tongues

moistened

sotziologuia

dripping into the eye

107.30

the place of their desire

     derived from

        to possess ultimativi

     they did not prroyect (the knowledge)

       of orrguani days

         one who augurs

           from the flight of birds

13.28

black spots on a white surface

white spots on a black surface

                                        koakah koalah brand mark

                      cauterizing iron

2.5

strengthen me

i.e., my blooz heart   with shocolaad apples

rafters of a categuorria

12.4

cellolarry struck brother lecondel on the heel

chorreographia

traces

carnival acclivity

clothes himself with shame is naked (none the less);"6
should be construed as the singular of עֲרוּמִים (Gn

ל

glanevrs לקט in לקטו (Ex 16.22) = لَقَطَ, "to pick, glean
לֶקֶט (Lv 19.9, 23.22) is similar to لُقْطَة and لُقَاطَة, "gle
fruit-trees that fell to the ground."[653]

לשן. לשון (Ex 4.10) = لِسَان, "tongue;" the H
denotes also "language," cf. Gn 10.5; Es 3.12, 8.9.[65
(Pr 30.10), מַלְשְׁנִי (Ps 101.5) are verbs derived from a
لَسَنَ, "to slander."[655]

Innocent
Abroad

How to shape sacred time

I can see easily enough that if I wish to profit
By this tour I must studiously and faithfully
Unlearn a great many things I have somehow absorbed
Concerning Palestine will ye render 79שׂ me a recompence?
And if ye recompense me speedily will I return
7ע25 upon your own head

I have purchased the right to access, must begin a system
Of reduction the magic recipe is therefore 'Anticipate,
Approach, Acknowledge, Afterthought' for whatsoever
Man that hath a blemish, she shall not approach
A blind 5787 or a lame 645ה or he that hath a flat
Nose or any thing superfluous 831ו

A willingness to endure loneliness, a relaxed way
With odd growths and unexplained fevers like my grapes
The spies bore out of the Promised Land everything
In Palestine on too large a scale separated
From thy bowels people stand 5975 upon the wall

The word 'Palestine' brought to mind a vague suggestion
Of a country as large as the U.S. breathtaking
Scenery, beautiful faces and unbelievable destruction
Shocked by the strain of displacement into significant
Experimentations written that thou mayest teach 3184 them

Some of my ideas were wild, prickly pears like hams
One could not say I failed to stretch out this
Very own body along the coast beside the sea, sinking
Bones into stones: a sardius, a topaz and a carbuncle
Behold I will lay 5414 stumbling blocks for
Mostly it's just cool to be in a place called catastrophe

Oriental scenes look best in not overly touristy steel
Engravings I must try to reduce my ideas of Palestine
To a more reasonable shape one gets large impressions
In boyhood she has to fight against all his life
All these kings 4ע28 that were with her and smote
52ב1 shall come out 3ר18 of thee

Messenger

We made a covenant of old with the Children of Israel and We sent unto them messengers. As often as a messenger came unto them with that which their souls desired not they became rebellious. Some they denied and some they slew.

We **took** the covenant of the Children of Israel and sent them **apostles**, every time, there came to them an apostle with what they themselves desired not – some (of these) they called impostors, and some they (**go so far** as to) **slay**.

Verily, We took the covenant of the Children of Israel and sent them Messengers. **Whenever** there came to them a Messenger with what they themselves desired not – a **group** of them they called liars, and others among them they killed.

Certainly We made a covenant with the children of Israel and We sent to them apostles; whenever there came to them an apostle with what that their souls **did** not desire, some (of them) did they call liars and some they slew.

Surely WE took a covenant from the Children of Israel, and WE sent Messengers to them. **But** every time there came to them a Messenger with what their **hearts** desired not, they **treated** some as liars, and some they **sought** to kill.

We have **taken** a covenant from the Children of Israel, and we sent to them messengers. Whenever a messenger went to them with anything they disliked, some of them they rejected, and some they killed.

And We took **compact** with the Children of Israel, and We sent Messengers to them. **Whensoever** there came to them a Messenger with that their souls had not desire for, some they **cried lies** to, and some they slew.

We took a compact of the children of Israel, and we sent to them apostles; every time there came to them an apostle with what their souls **loved** not, a **part** of them they did call liars and a part of them they slew.

Of old we accepted the covenant of the children of Israel, and sent Apostles to them. **Oft** as an Apostle came to them with that for which they had no desire, some they treated as liars, and some they slew;

We **formerly** accepted the covenant of the children of Israel, and sent apostles unto them. So often as an apostle came unto them with that which their souls desired not, they accused some of them of **imposture**, and some of them they killed:

La-qad akhadhnā mīthāqa Banī Isrā'īla wa-arsalnā ilayhim rusulan kulla-mā jā'ahum rasūlun bi-mā lā tahwā anfusuhum farīqan kadhdhabū wa-farīqan yaqtulūna. (5.70)

Jews in space (a lunacy)

Setting: Two women, age fifty to sixty-five, partially clad, in the locker room of the downtown 'Hebrew Y.'

Morocco is so beautiful – the mountains, the people. But what's this I hear about a new trip?

We can only do this covertly, quietly in December.

Good for you! How long?

Ten days we shall act like silent spies.

Only ten? … Not very much.

We shall spirit the penniless population across the border and out of this world we shall buy, buy, buy …

Yes, yes, but where is this lebensraum?

Israel has great spas and bomb shelters cum guestrooms, but you know the moon's the only place we're safe from anti-Semitism.

Aha! … Is it safe to go now?

Yes, and spas are much cheaper – Israelis own 10 percent of the moon already.

Then go! I imagine it will bring up philosophical thoughts about manifest destiny.

I was thinking of pitching a story to the *Globe*'s travel section so I can get it paid for.

Good for you! But you know … you'll need a unique angle when what matters isn't infinity but a language cleansed of all magic.

I'm going with my daughter, who's measuring dust flows above the Mediterranean.

There – you can write it from your perspective and her perspective.

And my niece, who's bringing a barbed-wire mezuzah, a dollar bill and a tiny Torah scroll from Bergen-Belsen.

That's your angle! Write it from your perspective, your daughter's perspective and your niece's perspective floating and looking at our peaceful planet while eating kosher nosh and reciting Israel's Declaration of Independence!

Jerusalem syndrome

It shares some features with the diagnostic category of a 'brief psychotic episode,' although a distinct progression of behaviours has been noted:

1. Anxiety, agitation and tension. We don't think in the holy places, we think in bed afterward, surfeited with sights.
2. Declaration of the intent to split off from the group or family and tour Jerusalem alone, the would-be messiahs, the misfits, the misguided, all flowering in the small hours. At this point, hotel personnel or tour guides may refer the tourist for psychiatric evaluation.
3. A need to be clean and pure: compulsive baths and showers, fingernail and toenail trimming. Our pilgrims' chief sin is their lust for 'specimens.'
4. Preparation, often with the aid of hotel bed linen, of an ankle-length, toga-like gown; a tall Arab, swarthy as an Indian, robe sweeping down a star-spangled banner of curved, sinuous bars of black and white.
5. What a relief to steal a procession or march to a holy place without a guide along to talk unceasingly about every stone you step upon and drag you back ages and ages to the day it achieved celebrity.
6. Public recitation, usually shouting or singing of loud Bible verses or spirituals. Adrenalin rises when you approach the *vicinity* and the *focus* is near egoic mental pain. Has it ever needed to hide its face?
7. Welcome, America! Yes, there are cowboys in JerUSAlem roping rough stubborn *Maxim* girls. How wearily the smouched ideas swarm about your path! The sermon is usually confused and based on an unrealistic plea to adopt a more wholesome, moral way of aren't IDF women the world's sexiest soldiers?

In the beginning he broke on his own initiative

I am a complex creative artist moving through walls
No picture left hanging, cupboards fall, my writing
Not intended for ordinary mortals in the U.S.
I am a mentor liberating panicked families
From house to house of thought

In the first house we took a Johnnie
For a neighbour procedure blown through
Autarkic swarm holes collecting inverse stuff
Geometry ensuring nothing fractal booby-
Trapped manoeuvres inside rooms before you
Do Germania so if a terrorist's inside Chicago
He would be hurt and not you, war
A matter of reading actually he is doing
Systemic searches smoothing out
The urban environment maybe even
Translating I don't know what, this hero
In a permanently coalescing space on his own
Initiative totally 5 kg hammer logic to conceal
Form you operate but not by presence
D & G a little too opaque kind of routine each
Time a house addressed in incomprehensible
Language took the hammer and we would watch
The reorganization of urban syntax

Only in retrospective I thought rosh katan
Discharge left Johnnie in and of the drift
Unwalling the law not from a love
For Israel will never understand the rival
System kills you as a guest

L'amiral cherche une maison à louer

Once there was a single Ein Houd
Now there are many versions
How could any of us escape that deadly layering?
How could we have failed to be grotesque?

Negrigrigrigriiiillons 7838 hair 8181 children 1\21 suck 3243
In it dans les nuuuuu a aaaages 5645 and thick darkness 282ב
I hoped to find a 'Tahiti' like Gauguin for my painting
Has Dada ever spoken to you about sleeping with Israel?
How happy I felt as I left the Ministry of Absorption
Bearing a new name OVERTURNED BY WHOM? DADA
One shouldn't let many words out je déchiiiiiiiire
Dogs 361\ and the fowls 57ז5 of the heaven
The key to a house and a small suitcase
Someone walks on your feet. It's Dada

Janco wore the Persian shaykh pants in the former mosque
Cum Café Voltaire, le geste gratuit
A protean state of mind where yes and no unsplit
At street corners, like dogs and grasshoppers
And the beasts 929 of the earth 7ע6 to devour and destroy la
Colliiiiiiiiiiiii 202ב and twelve pillarsine le tapiiii ii iii iii is
We witnessed the desert and its smoothed out music
'Abandoned Arab village' un objet trouvé
Replete with scenes of Biblical desolation
THE HOLY VIRGIN WAS ALREADY A DADAIST
Mrs. Janco mourned the pleasing decay of another ruin

We demanded the tabula rasa Dada
Covers things with an artificial gentleness, the Police
Of the Police manifested only in violent Dada m'dada acts
If all pills are Pink Pills a virgin microbe penetrates
Small blue and white pottery dish in the door
With the insistence of air Janco dances 4246 saying 5°9
Saul hath slain 52ב1 his thousands and David his ten
723ר to his own boomboom boomboom boomboom
Each Negro mask demanding an appropriate costume
Smote 52ב1 and discomfited thee an ark of gopher
Set of gestures close to madness, paradox
Triumphed as the feeling grew: forbidden
To touch the non-native pine trees killing the olive
Pawnshop mhm Dada the white cat miaows
Lawns and flowers all collapses somehow
Dada Dalai Lama, Buddha, Bible and Nietzsche
Air in the house hard to da homo da
Halo of place halo of sumūd da sacer da
World's best lily-milk soap das Ding m'dada
Don't want words other people have invented
Sold in the museum in homage de Duchamp
I am here accidentally

ABC fulminates against 1, 2, 3 to disseminate
Little abcs and big abcs in a form absolute
Why can't a tree be called 6086 Pluplusch
Un graaaaaaaaaand dead neighbour the ideal
Sexual partner shall pay double 79שׂ of a tolerant
Lesbia regula can't take it over, it kind of takes over
Let's change one letter only in Palimpstine
You kind of crawl into somebody else's 5315 soul
Leave philosophy in a rage and sharpen
Your wings and their 64ːo faces shall conquer
An art studio asleep all the gold of earth and sun
And all the people shall say 5ה9 jouissance
Or thanatourism cursed 7ע9 the ground
In sorrow shalt thou eat thy search for India
Glory Springs in the place of Trough Springs
Distressed creature 5315 panaaaaaaankaa
Present absentees like ghosts as it was in Dada neee ma teeechnintes et yayayaya
tagaaa a aaan insomnie inie iaoai xixixi xixi cla cla clo
drrrrrrrrrrrrrrrrrrrrrrrrrrrrr the rest is
one-legged
sauce

Talkback

Shugga makes an all too common error in stating you're a voice that matters

The guiding principles of the talkback forum will be mutual respect and an openness to generations of tsouris it's 1959 all over again, or 969 or 1979 or 1989 or 1999! It's 1959 all over again, or 969 or 1979 or 1989 or 1999!

shugga, I have no idea what motivates you as long as men are willing to demonetize one another what happened to the Native Americans was going to happen at some point like *Groundhog Day* replete with blood and death

Participants, even if they oppose coexistence, must, within the confines, a boy walks through the rubble strumming on a broken oud thinking why palestine, why not somewhere else … baja, california, perhaps … take the whole damn peninsula … we'll work out the details with mexico

SHUGGA--there is NOTHING to be discussed hebrew and arabic writing are both pretty looking serious talks might begin if both sides used the ('epoche') of husserl with the god thing shit with time and patience censorship is an unapologetic mulberry leaf all our ingenuity a silk gown

SHUGGA--- What a Hypocite/LIAR YOU ARE! Political orientation has no bearing if I keep a green bough in my heart HAVE YOU SHUGGA EVER TOLD THE TRUTH IN YOUR LIFE???????????? it often seems like events clash with their own interpretation who taught you to LIE, LIE and LIE?????? ?????? Calling you names is worthless vicodin in the water system/get them to forget for a year/because you have NO SHAME/get every one to go to sleep basically WORTHLESS!

Sugar-- Sugar Baby--- When you go outside watch the weather if there is no third path when you come inside watch people's faces and the singing bird will come that is the one we are going to take in the meantime I bleed for the victims of all sides don't pull down the fences

SWEETIE PIE SUGAR-------Have a good one! Nighty NITE! shalom

Grounds for deletion

1. Racist remarks, as well as slurs on the basis of religion, ethnicity and gender.
2. Use of the terms Nazi, Hitler, ethnic cleansing, to describe the actions and policies of Israelis or Palestinians.
3. Personal attacks, vulgarities and profanities directed at other participants in the forum. Hang in there, Shugga!
4. If you are patient in one moment of anger you will escape 100 days of advocacy of violence against individuals or religious, ethnic or racial groups.
5. Use of the phrase 'There are no Palestinians' or derivatives thereof. It is only when the cold season comes that we notice the pine and cypress to be ever green.

Acknowledgement

The third point creates a space rather than a line
The experience when you come face to face
With the *focus*, not just in the *vicinity*
The milk coming from an outside breast, not me

Buber took Said's home with a deed from the Jewish Agency
Life owes me reparation and I will see that I get it
Drawing a line between inside and outside
They love their delusions as they love themselves
For they are exceptions and intend to remain so

Here we go round the prickly pear
Terminology the properly poetic moment of thought
It's only because we can count to three
That we can count to two

The Levite and the Cohen pass by the injured man
Stop where you are and acknowledge its presence
With the section marked Acknowledgement
We who live are also always killing Hey you!
The poem already exists before it is written

Lévinas stands watch over the Shoah
Ethics suspended at the border crossing
Dream of virgin lands and arctic snows
A world without difference, textuality
It is never just me and the event

Philosophy chokes on a small fragment
Some strange Zug in the Muselmann's face
A bit of microeconomics, the person
Here I am a debt that can never be amortized

Undecidability stops in the fractal space
Between I and Thou, the killing and dying
Unthinkable truth of living experience
Only the unforgivable can be proximity
Taking a new meaning in the landscape
Of contiguity

Mixed crowd

And We said unto the Children of Israel after him: Dwell in the land;
but when the promise of the Hereafter cometh to pass We shall bring
you as a crowd gathered out of various nations.

And We said thereafter to the Children of Israel, 'Dwell **securely** in
the land (of promise)': but when the **second** of the **warnings came** to
pass, We gathered you **together** in a **mingled** crowd.

And We said to the Children of Israel after him: 'Dwell in the land,
then, when the **final** and the last promise **comes near** (i.e. the Day of
Resurrection or the descent of **Christ, son** of **Mary on** the **earth**) We
shall bring you altogether as mixed crowd (gathered out of various
nations).

And We said to the Israelites after him: Dwell in the land: and when
the promise of the **next life** shall come to pass, we will bring you both
together in judgment.

And after him WE said to the Children of Israel, Dwell **ye** in the
promised land; and when the time of the promise of the Latter Days
comes, WE shall bring you together out of various **peoples**.

And we said to the Children of Israel afterwards, '**Go live into this**
land. When the final prophecy comes to pass, we will summon you all
in one group.'

And We said to the Children of Israel after him, 'Dwell in the land;
and when the promise of the world to come comes to pass, We shall
bring you a **rabble**.'

And after him we said to the children of Israel, 'Dwell ye in the land;
and when the promise of the hereafter comes to pass, we will bring
you in a mixed crowd (to judgment).'

And after his death, we said to the children of Israel, 'Dwell ye in the land:' and when the promise of the next life shall come to pass, we will bring you both **up** together to judgment.

And we said unto the children of Israel, after (his destruction), dwell ye in the land: And when the promise of the next life shall come (to **be fulfilled**), we will bring you (both) **promiscuously** (to judgement).

Wa-qulnā min baʿdihi li-Banī Isrāʾīla: Uskunu 'l-arda fa-idhā jāʾa waʿdu 'l-Akhīrati jiʾnā bi-kum lafifan. (17.104)

Anticipate (peut-être)

Was Walter Benjamin 1\4ז all these things against me the first suicide
Bomber carrying all his cattle, all his 739ז goods, a book
Of Hebrew grammar, this 37ז8 babbler a setter forth
Of strange 1\40 gods a pathological vacillation

Did *The Human Condition* and *Battlestar Galactica* arise
Walk through the 7ז6 land in the length of the
Breadth of the binational state's 2572 cubits
Failure less a body of work 439ז she made than an action
I wish I could run the five-fingered comb through your frizzy hair

Odradek and the little hunchback poets say we are 2070 also 2532
Our offspring present a special risk to national security out of sheer passion
They'd never do harm because my soul's 3ז65 precious to a fly

Configurations on the sky strong as a molten 3רז2 looking glass
Something like the rustling 510· of falling allegorists
Catastrophic spell of the hump things assume in oblivion
Contradictory and mobile whole scraps at daybreak

The state of emergency is no longer the hasbara
But the de la teeee ee erre moooooonte swerve that trips up thought
My penny in the slot made a slight adjustment
Like wayside robbers relieving the idle stroller des bouuuules
Of 49 levels of meaning to sail the 51א7 coasts of Asia

Somehow is the stamp of a point of view making 3835 brick now
Somehow Angelus Novus shouldn't hang over the backside of the tabernacle
In the Israel as a prince hast thou power Museum
Count 7ע16 for the lamb off our crepuscular blushes
Like a collection notice oussent les clarinettes for paradise

Never trust what writers say about standing alone
1א4ſ Benjamin needed instruction to hold a cup of hot tea
O my friends, there is a friend hast stricken thy hand with a stranger
The book and she shall blot 42ɔ9 is more important than la suuu uurfa
aaa aace

31° 45′ 21.77″ N

34° 39′ 30.30″ E

L'éveil

Day Two

they caught us with our pants down	
	a naked woman tucks herself
no identifiable body	
	into the Arabic seen
we feel weak now	
	Buy $
destroying	the Islamist genie
turn back the clock	framed with glowing white sparks
I don't suggest conquering	
	to jaw-jaw is better than
	to war-war
deadliest day of the conflict	high chalky spine of the
(since last year)	(nobody's calling for reservations
nine members of the Salmiyeh family	
	an act of war
	restrained but very, very, very
famously denied the	painful
Holocaust	air strikes coupled with rhetoric
residents gave out sweets	wardens heard cries of joy
hugging and kissing for Abdullah and Wiesel	like all good theatre the story
	is the bulk of the
perverse momentum of its own	work

Day Three

rhetorical escalation

our field of action large

our actions diverse

every tree a target

measured

first her head

unequivocal

then her arms

itching

torn pages rustled eerily in hot wind

signed, Israel

language added

it sometimes seems that time

collapsed

blurring the lines between root
causes   and consequences

if your position
a full page

I mean it's a resort, not a war zone

how can you make it into a sticker?

quiet as the panic buying ended

each of our soldiers pure gold

I thought you were going to ask

I don't want anything
to breathe

about the pig

Day Four

a hammer to kill a fly   let us open our associations

the other cheek
is not   look into the middle of the sea

logical, not hysterical   we will go beyond and beyond

Iran a nasty look

(look at it burning)

not a passionate summer fling   uncalculated adventure

common field of
emotions

poster boys of Muhammad
and Ali

swallowed a cancer
and must vomit up

how many Arabs for each
Israeli

who needs peace when you have

America

Day Five

this is my first war

I will not ask you for your history   only the birds outside

all the prophet's household   clutching her befurred microphone

not carte blanche but a clean table   the robot bomb probe waltzed

back into the gyre   one for a baby, two a road accident

with folded hands   the family playing host to the missile

deal the cards yourself   it's in the DNA

Afterthought

'Shoot & Weep' and 'Book of Comparisons' were drafted in 2007–2008, then transformed after my first visit to Israel-Palestine. Waiting for my flight to Tel Aviv in a Toronto airport lounge just before midnight on December 31, 2008, I watched CBC Newsworld's scenes of 'bloodbath in Gaza,' while listening to a group of young adults behind me prepare for their free Birthright Israel trip by playing a game called 'Two Truths and a Lie.' I'm not sure if I ever can or want to put into words what happened during my time in Israel-Palestine. Instead, I have inserted some of the journey's mad affects into this book.

'Shoot & Weep' emerges from numerous print and online sources of testimony, statistics, theory, story, fact and myth, including the HESEG (Lone Soldier) Foundation, funded by billionaire Canadian bookseller Heather Reisman and her husband. 'Grievable' invokes Judith Butler and Federico García Lorca and attaches names to the circumstances in 'Did not participate in hostilities'; 'Nominal' attaches ages to the people in 'Grievable.' To paraphrase Thomas Hobbes, power is the 'capacity to give names and enforce definitions.' Former Israeli General Moshe Dayan said, speaking of the 418 Palestinian villages destroyed in 1948, 'You do not even know the names of these Arab villages, and I do not blame you, because those geography books no longer exist.' 'The capacity to give names' should be repeated twelve times with names, verbs and predicates replaced, e.g., 'Gonen sapped the foundations of Ghuraba/Meron cut up Mirun's root and branch/Sasa made mincemeat of Sa'sa'/Chuqoq scattered Yaquq to the winds,' and so on, with a remainder of two lines left unvoiced. A *dīwān* is a traditional guesthouse, formerly at the centre of Palestinian communal life.

'Book of Comparisons' is based on eleventh-century Andalusian Jewish scholar Ibn Barun's 'Book of Comparison' of common verbal roots and similar phrases in the sister Semitic languages of classical Arabic and Hebrew as a method of Biblical translation and exegesis. The words in each segment of the poem appear in the same order as they do in the root entries in Pinchas Wechter's English translation of Ibn Barun's masterwork (originally written in Arabic). A few English loan words used in Modern Hebrew also appear, partly as an impure gesture to the de-Arabization of the Hebrew language in its modern incarnation. Among the many new coinages in Modern Hebrew (any word that wasn't in the Bible had to be coined), *cellolarry* seems to mean 'cellular' and *lecondel* is a slang take on former U.S. Secretary of State Condoleezza Rice. According to the online Double-Tongued Dictionary, 'People say that they don't have time to "lecondel" – meaning to come and go for meetings that produce few results.' 'Book of Comparisons' transformed in tandem with the progress of my unknowing and is most recently indebted to a statement by Jacques Derrida: '[F]ar from being the beginning of pure ethics, the neighbour as like [*le prochain comme semblable*] or as resembling, as looking like, spells the end or the ruin of such an ethics, if there is any.'

There are numbers in a few 'Innocent Abroad' poems that are also word values in the online Blue Letter Bible concordance. For word values with consecutive repeated numbers (e.g., 7725), either the Hebrew letter or Arabic numeral for the repeated number is inserted and voiced. For word values that contain two of the same number, but non-consecutively (e.g., 5787), the Hebrew name for the repeated (Arabic) number is voiced (i.e., 'five-seven-eight-*sheva*'). (Please see the Pronunciation Key on page 85.) 'Messenger' and 'Mixed crowd' employ multiple English translations of Qur'ān passages as found via the online YaQuB: Yet Another Qur'ān Browser. 'Jews in space' draws on a number of true stories, including an account of what the first Israeli in space, Ilan Ramon, brought with him on the fateful Columbia voyage in 2003, and a newspaper article on Israelis buying up plots on the moon. Some explication of the Jerusalem Syndrome can be found in the *Lonely Planet Guide to Israel & the Palestinian Territories* and in the DSM-IV under Culture-Bound Syndromes, including Ghost Sickness, Old Hag Syndrome and Brain Fag.

Israel's recent branding or *hasbara* ('overseas image-building') campaigns are intriguing, including a photo spread in the men's magazine *Maxim* on Israel Defense Forces (IDF) women soldiers. Chicago is the name of the mock-up town in the Negev desert that the IDF uses to perform urban warfare training manoeuvres, some based on concepts pilfered from Deleuze and Guattari and the Situationists. Germania was a curious IDF code name for the Jenin refugee camp, a site of fierce Palestinian resistance. Eyal Weizman's book, *Hollow Land: Israel's Architecture of Occupation*, is an important source, as is the Breaking the Silence: Israeli Soldiers Talk About the Occupied Territories website. Among the testimonies on Breaking the Silence is one soldier describing the 'neighbour procedure' – the IDF use of Palestinians as human shields, including forcing Palestinians to break walls inside their neighbours' homes, so that the army can move literally through the walls from house to house. The IDF name for these neighbours became 'Johnnies' during Operation Cast Lead in Gaza (named 'Cast Lead' after a famous children's Hanukkah poem, because the Operation started during the Festival of Lights in December 2008, and some very special dreidels are made from cast lead). 'Unwalling the law' is a partial palindrome of U.S. artist Gordon Matta-Clark's practice of 'unwalling the wall.' *Rosh katan* is Hebrew for 'small head.' The Double-Tongued Dictionary defines it as 'an attitude of avoiding responsibility, of extreme self-interest, or of strict adherence to rules to the point of obstruction or absurdity ... The term seems to have arisen in the Israeli military.'

Susan Slyomovics' book, *The Object of Memory: Arab and Jew Narrate the Palestinian Village*, tells the story of Dadaist Marcel Janco founding a Dada artists' community in 1953 in what was Palestinian Ein Houd ('Trough Springs' in Arabic). Janco and company changed the village name to Ein Hod ('Glory Springs' in Hebrew). A remnant of Ein Houd's former inhabitants (those not in Jenin camp or farther exile) formed an adjacent 'unrecognized' village named Ein Houd al-Jadidah (New Ein Houd). *Sumūd* is Arabic for steadfastness. Mahmoud Darwish's 'Indian Speech,' Tristan Tzara's 'La Panka' and a few Dada manifestos are intertexts. Palimpstine is an imaginary land coined by Salman Rushdie in *The Moor's Last Sigh*, a place 'where worlds collide, flow in and out of one another ... Under World beneath Over World, black market beneath white.'

According to *The German Ideology*, 'Philosophy and the study of the actual world have the same relation to one another as masturbation and sexual love.' *Works of Love* deems the dead neighbour tolerably fuckable, while Hillel delivers a one-legged neighbour one-liner. Aristotle's *Lesbia regula* – justice as pliable rule – is invoked, 'For the rule of what is indefinite is also indefinite, like the leaden rule used in Lesbian architecture; the rule changes to fit the shape of the stone and does not remain a rule.' I recently penned an almost sincere manifesto called 'Poesis by the Lesbia Regula.' For Erasmus, 'by the Lesbian rule ... is said when things are done the wrong way round, when theory is accommodated to fact and not fact to theory, when law is suited to conduct, not conduct corrected by law.' According to Renaissance scholar Paula Blank, 'the lesbian rule perverts rather than promotes the discovery of "truth."'

Comment sections to blog and online article posts can be fascinating and disturbing, and this can be the case on Jewlicious.com, Haaretz.com, Boston.com (*The Boston Globe* online) and a Silliman's Blog post on Operation Cast Lead. The Museum on the Seam for Dialogue, Understanding and Coexistence in Jerusalem has interesting fridge magnets for sale, including 'If I keep a green bough in my heart the singing bird will come.' Jacqueline Rose entered *The Question of Zion* by paraphrasing Russian formalist Victor Shklovsky, 'There is no third path and that is the one we are going to take.'

After the massacres in the Sabra and Shatila refugee camps in 1982, a journalist asked Emmanuel Lévinas: 'For the Israeli, isn't the "other" above all the Palestinian?' Lévinas replied: 'My definition of the other is completely different. The other is the neighbour, who is not necessarily kin, but who can be. And in that sense, if you're for the other, you're for the neighbour. But if your neighbour attacks another neighbour or treats him unjustly, what can you do? Then alterity takes on another character, in alterity we can find an enemy, or at least we are faced with the problem of knowing who is right and who is wrong, who is just and who is unjust. There are people who are wrong.' Indeed there are.

Michael Taussig is responsible for the rather explosive 'Was Walter Benjamin the first suicide bomber?' I'm moved by Derrida's profane 'messianic hope ... without content,' which can manifest itself as an urgent injunction to act in the present, much as democracy or justice à venir may never come. Chips of Benjamin's own messianic 'now-time' (jetztzeit) also flash up as unarchived, effaced remembrances of suffering that interrupt and reorient this time. Gershon (formerly Gerhard) Scholem wrote, 'Somehow is the stamp of a point of view in the making,' adding that he'd never heard anyone use the word 'somehow' more frequently than his friend Benjamin. Benjamin vacillated for years about whether to learn Hebrew and join Scholem in then-British Palestine. I too have experienced an uncanny aversion to Modern Hebrew, barely progressing beyond its aleph-bet. 'I wish I could run the five-fingered comb through your frizzy hair' is Martin Heidegger's love sigh to Hannah Arendt, and could also be a plaintive call in the face of the unreadable. I am indebted to a statement from *The Neighbor: Three Inquiries in Political Theology* (Žižek, Santer, Reinhard): 'If you do not want to talk about Odradek, Gregor Samsa and the *Muselmann*, then shut up about your love for a neighbor.'

'L'éveil' comprises four remnants of an otherwise abandoned poem on Israel's thirty-three-day war in Lebanon that started July 12, 2006 and was my original awakening to this project. The poem was to be thirty-three pages long and in a four-square 'war map,' containing language from daily war coverage in the *Globe and Mail* (top left), *Lebanon Daily Star* (top right), *New York Times* (bottom left), and *Jerusalem Post* (bottom right) – Canada and Lebanon both being northern neighbours to 'supersized' southern presences. These few days were reclaimed in January 2009 in Jerusalem – it seemed appropriate somehow.

Pronunciation key

Hebrew letter for number (archaic)	Hebrew name for letter/ number	Arabic numeral	Hebrew for Arabic numeral	Arabic number (script)	Arabic name for number
		0	efes	.	sifr
א	Aleph	1	akhat	١	*waa*-hed
ב	Bet	2	shtai'im	٢	ith-*nayn*
ג	Gimmel	3	shalosh	٣	ta-*laa*-te
ד	Dalet	4	arba	٤	'ar-ba'
ה	Hei	5	khamesh	٥	*kham*-se
ו	Vav	6	shesh	٦	*sit*-te
ז	Zayin	7	sheva	٧	*sab*-'a
ח	Chet	8	shmone	٨	ta-*maa*-ni-ya
ט	Tet	9	tesha	٩	tis-'a

Acknowledgements

Abundant thanks to Kevin Connolly, Rachel Levitsky, Bob Majzels, and especially Kate Eichhorn and Margaret Christakos, for close readings of this work and excellent suggestions that changed its shape for the better.

Thank you to Alana, Christina, Evan, Stan, Rick and the Coach House printers for continuing to labour tirelessly to make beautiful books.

For a variety of generous acts in relation to this project, my sincere gratitude to: Ammiel Alcalay, Sandra Alland, Elena Basile, Charles Bernstein, Joel Bettridge, Judith Butler, Sami Shalom Chetrit, Moyra Davey, Thom Donovan, Sarah Dowling, Natasha Dudinski, Laura Elrick, Rob Fitterman, Dina Georgis, Lyn Hejinian, Jerusalem Hotel, RM Kennedy, Jacqueline Larson, Nathanaël, M. NourbeSe Philip, Meredith and Peter Quartermain, Kim Rosenfield, Tamer Salaseh, Kaia Sand, Heidi Schaefer, Leonard Schwartz, Cheryl Sourkes, Juliana Spahr, Rodrigo Toscano, Mark Twain and b.h. Yael.

Special thanks to Kathy Wazana, for invaluable advice and assistance regarding my travel to Israel-Palestine; David Larsen, for correcting the Arabic orthography errors in the text; Nathan Kensinger, for the evocative cover image; Bryan Gee, for the beautiful cover design; and Elle Flanders and Tamira Sawatzky, for the image on p. 74, a cross-hair from a photograph of the former Palestinian village of Isdud referencing its longitude and latitude marks. *What Isn't There* is an ongoing installation documenting the absent presence of destroyed Palestinian villages.

Earlier versions of certain poems appeared in *Gam, Abraham Lincoln, Wheelhouse, Interim, Ottawater* and in a Kelly Writers House broadside and a Dia at the Hispanic Society pamphlet. The first manifestation of *Shoot & Weep* was published as a chapbook by Nomados Literary Publishers. Some poems are also in the anthology *Prismatic Publics: Innovative Canadian Women's Poetry and Poetics* (Coach House) and a forthcoming anthology of conceptual writing from Les Figues Press. Many thanks to all of the editors.

This project was made possible with the support of a Chalmers Arts Fellowship and grants from the Ontario Arts Council Writers' Works in Progress and Writers' Reserve programs, and the Toronto Arts Council.

This book is for Kate, for dreaming a bigger life with me.

About the Author

Rachel Zolf is a poet and editor from Toronto who is presently living in New York. *Human Resources* (Coach House Books) won the 2008 Trillium Book Award for Poetry and was a finalist for a Lambda Award. Previous collections include *Shoot & Weep* (Nomados), *from Human Resources* (Belladonna books), *Masque* (The Mercury Press) and *Her absence, this wanderer* (BuschekBooks).

Typeset in Arno
Printed and bound at the Coach House on bpNichol Lane, 2010

Edited by Kevin Connolly
Cover design by Bryan Gee
Cover photograph by Nathan Kensinger, courtesy of the photographer
Image, p. 74, from *What Isn't There* by Flanders & Sawatzky, courtesy of the artists
Author photo by Elena Basile

Coach House Books
80 bpNichol Lane
Toronto on M5S 3J4

416 979 2217
800 367 6360

mail@chbooks.com
www.chbooks.com